£.1

THE N~
MED

THE NEW MEDIUMSHIP

GRACE COOKE

THE WHITE EAGLE PUBLISHING TRUST
LISS · HAMPSHIRE · ENGLAND

First published October 1965
Sixth impression May 1994

© *Copyright, The White Eagle Publishing Trust, 1965*

ISBN 0-85487-068-7

Printed in Great Britain by
Cambridge University Press

Contents

FOREWORD
By Sir Ronald Fraser

It ought to be recognised at this time of day that there are among us people, sometimes called 'sensitives,' who live in a state of consciousness that is subtler, wider in scope, than what we usually mean when we say we are conscious. It ought to be known that, whatever the cruder manifestations of Spiritualism may have amounted to, 'seeing' is a genuine operation of the psyche and yields authentic intelligence about this world and others. There are people, that is to say, who make conscious use of mechanisms not open to surgical investigation but susceptible of inspection by clear sight, organs of experience which when fully awakened and under control yield perceptions that are at present beyond the range of the rest of us. Such a one is the writer of this book.

It has been a privilege to receive from White Eagle, over a number of years, through Mrs. Grace Cooke, continuous and systematic instruction on the nature of reality and the way to reach it. It has been a privilege to receive, on occasion, advice that was shrewd, stimulating, sometimes cryptic and always directed to an end beyond one's personal convenience. In the first place, all he says gives immediacy, not to say urgency, living truth, to theologies and theogonies that we have inherited from the past, whether Indian, Chinese or Egyptian, Hermetic or

Gnostic; moreover, it throws a sudden bright light onto sayings of Jesus and events in his life that have not been well understood. In the second place, he teaches a way of conduct, a discipline, that does more than enable us to get through the day without succumbing to our troubles; it develops the latent faculties of our humanity and must lead in time to the self-realisation, the liberation of self from itself, that has been the aim of all systems.

In order to communicate what he would say to a world in dire need of it, and to effect the purposes of certain exalted spirits for whom he speaks sometimes, White Eagle has associated with himself an old acquaintance, a 'sensitive,' a 'medium,' who by a life of rigorous self-discipline, a life of aspiration, meditation and the exercise of practical ability in the conduct of affairs, has with the devoted aid of those nearest her been able to accomplish something far beyond what was envisaged in the early days of Spiritualism, something outside the range of those who are as it might be said slightly psychic. It is to her that we owe our contact with White Eagle's strong, sane personality, the gift of his instruction and much else.

I

EARLY DAYS

Man has always hoped or tried to believe that his soul will survive death. Early attempts by people on the 'Other Side' to prove their existence consisted of raps on a table, or knocks in other parts of a room, some very loud indeed. After the knocks and raps came the production of 'materialised' forms clothed in 'ectoplasm,' followed by many other forms of so-called 'physical' phenomena; in time these were replaced by mental transmission or telepathy, through which messages from the 'dead' were given to the living. A crude and rather clumsy form of this reception was first introduced through the 'planchette,' a little triangle of wood mounted on two wheels, with a pencil at one corner. This contraption could run about freely on a large sheet of paper and write messages which sometimes were long and evidential.

This was a step forward, if only a small one. Soon it was found unnecessary to use a planchette, as the mind of the would-be medium could itself receive impressions and write them down. In this way 'inspirational' messages, as they are called, 'came through,' and even 'automatic writing' messages, in which the hand holding the pencil took itself along without the owner of that hand knowing what it wrote until afterwards. Sometimes both hands could be so employed while the medium was reading a book,thus emphasising the 'automatic' character of the writing. My sister used to do this, but hers was 'mirror' or 'backwards' writing, unreadable until held before a mirror.

For the past sixty years I myself have been closely associated with the practice of mediumship, and during this period have witnessed and taken part in nearly every type of psychic experiment including materialisation, psychic photography, telekinesis, direct voice mediumship and trumpet manifestations. I have also experienced many forms of mental mediumship in which are included diagnosis, healing, trance control, clairvoyance, clairaudience and telepathy.

Physical mediumship has been the means of convincing many scientists and materialists that we survive death and has shown the power which is in a medium to demonstrate communication between the living and the dead; but I am of the opinion that physical phenomena can be dangerous in the hands of an amateur and ought to be confined to the laboratory and supervised by experts.

Psychic phenomena have been changing during the last twenty-five years, and we have seen a gradual strengthening and development of the *mental* side of mediumship. The demonstration of this psychic power through spiritual healing, for instance, is making a considerable impact upon the scepticism of many churchmen, doctors and religious groups as well as laymen. Remarkable demonstrations of clairvoyance and clairaudience, as well as the impressive manifestation of trance-control by spirits bringing deeper knowledge and understanding of life's meaning and purpose, are attracting interest among all classes; not least among young people of both sexes, who perhaps are better equipped mentally than their parents were to think for themselves about the mysteries of life and death. They seek not so much physical proof as a logical explanation of man's undoubted psychic powers and what they portend.

Psychologists and psychiatrists have come near to discovering the existence of a higher consciousness in man; yet in spite of their work I believe that the potentialities inherent in the human soul have scarcely been explored, and a vast field of investigation into man's psychic powers and the scientific and moral laws which underlie and govern his conscious, subconscious and superconscious self awaits us today.

An extract from the editorial of the *Evening News* of Friday, January 25th, 1963, makes this same point:—

'One subject that forever intrigues, mystifies and baffles the mind of man is—the mind of man.

'Only the other day we learned that Russian and British research groups will attempt to transmit thought by telepathy between Britain and Russia under the auspices of the Cambridge University Society for Research into Parapsychology.

'The study of psychic phenomena is far from new. The ancients had their soothsayers, diviners, necromancers and wizards. But until recent years the whole matter was the domain of superstition rather than of science. Even today it is too often confused and debased by charlatanry.

'But under modern conditions, hard-headed scientists all over the world are experimenting and researching into the unknown capacities of the human mind and are achieving some astonishing results, inexplicable on any recognised hypothesis and mathematically beyond coincidence.

'In many ways such studies are more important than the exploration of space: they are more likely to produce directly useful results—and infinitely less costly.

'It is good to know that the universities are encouraging a branch of science that they did not even recognise as existing a few years ago—and that they are reaching out to co-operate with overseas faculties.

'For this is a subject so vast and so profound that the small isolated units which have hitherto dedicated themselves to its study could not hope to get far beyond the fringe of discovery.'

It may well be, as the editorial says, that man is on the fringe of immense discoveries concerning his own spiritual nature. If people will investigate with patience, perseverance and goodwill they will surely progress toward some marvellous discovery revealing (among other wonders) the continuation of human life in a fascinating spirit world.

When I was only seven years old my

mother's death made me aware of another world, a 'fairy land' as I used to call it. I would listen to my elder sisters and brothers talking about messages my father had received from my dead mother, and about people who had spoken to them from another life. I remember so well, frequently hearing what 'Starshine' had said and what my mother had come back to say about what we should do and how we should live if we wanted to grow up happy and useful to other people. I remember also a nice little boy called Jackie who used to tell me about a fairy world that was very real to him and how, if *we* died, we should probably go to this lovely place. I remember staying in the home of the daughter of one of my father's friends and how normal and natural it seemed when we went to bed each night to be told by her to move up and leave room for Dickie, her brother, to lie by her side. Dickie was a baby brother who had just died; and this little girl talked to and about him so naturally, not just believing, but *knowing* that he was alive and came to see her every night.

I grew up with this kind of simple belief and trust and so became very familiar with the spirit world.

When my mother died she left my father

with eight children, so it was natural that in a few years he should marry a second time. My stepmother was a wonderful 'psychic', and we had many demonstrations of the presence of invisible friends in the home. I remember how her Indian guide, while she was in trance, would pick up red-hot coals from the burning fire, hold them, and try to pass them on to us to hold. We were never courageous enough to accept his proffered gift, although he assured us it would not burn us. When my stepmother came out of her trance she would find her hands blackened by the burning coals, but the skin and flesh were quite normal and unburnt.

This guide seemed to be expert in controlling fire, for on another occasion he promised to give us a demonstration of how to suspend the burning away of coal; and as on the next day we were going out for many hours, suggested we should not replenish the fire. 'Leave it exactly as it is,' the guide said, 'I promise you it will be the same when you return.' Just as we went out a torn piece of paper was thrown on the fire, which curled into a black sheet. When we returned nine or ten hours later, we found that, true to the Indian's promise, the fire was exactly as it had been. The curled, blackened paper still lay on top while the coal did not appear to have burned away at all. I don't know if there can be any known physical reason for this, but it certainly occurred and I have no explanation for this curious phenomenon other than the one given by our Indian friend. I have actually seen a gas burner with a very stiff tap turned up to full power by an unseen hand.

My first *personal* communication came one night when I was left alone in a detached house some distance away from its neighbour. Being only thirteen or fourteen years old, I was naturally scared to hear heavy footsteps in my bedroom overhead. However, I summoned courage to go upstairs to investigate, only to find the room empty and untouched. Yet I was sure that I had heard those footsteps pacing to and fro. I was familiar with the story of the Fox sisters in America, who had got into communication with the spirit of a travelling pedlar who had been murdered in the house in which they were then living, and his body buried in the cellar beneath. I knew that he had given them all this information by answering their questions by means of a code of raps on the wall. The story was later investigated and found to be true. So with this story in mind I started mentally to ask the originator of the mysterious footsteps who he was, and by the same code of knockings, 'they' spelt out an intelligible reply. They had come, they said, to reassure me; they told me not to be nervous of being alone in an empty house, because I was being guarded and would be protected by the Indian friend whom by this time I knew quite well.

In those early years I became very familiar with invisible friends and came to regard them as companions who took a kindly interest in my life, and gave wise advice if need arose. This gentle care and watchfulness has never ceased throughout my life and many extraordinary and to some people unbelievable events have come about through their wise guidance. Sometimes it has been through a series of unconscious changes, when it seemed as though an unknown gentle power was slowly but definitely pushing me in a certain direction, perhaps to meet people, or to take me to a particular place where events occurred which at the time seemed unimportant but whose subsequent outcome proved quite marvellous and even miraculous.

May I add that I have also known 'them' to *prevent* me from going to a place which was unhealthy from a psychic angle by simply using someone else to make me miss the only available train. This occurred when I had arranged to visit a haunted house at a time when engaged on more important work. Had I gone as I had planned, it would have interfered with the reception of certain valuable communications at that time being given through me. Such happenings taught me to respect the precision of the psychic laws which govern communication with life in the next world, and how necessary it is for any would-be psychic to know exactly what can or cannot be done by someone who hopes to become an etheric bridge between the two worlds of life.

In my book *Plumed Serpent** (which tells the story of a past incarnation of mine in South America) I have described my early training in these mysteries, and how my (then) brother and I became initiated into a priestly order officiating in the Temple of the Great White Light. At that time, although people were not so advanced scientifically as they are today, much of their time was devoted to the awakening, growth and understanding of the inner powers of the soul—'occult powers' they are called today, meaning powers which work on the inner or unseen planes of life.

The instruction given to me during that

* Now incorporated in *The Illumined Ones*.

early incarnation has remained within my soul and has slowly developed throughout subsequent incarnations. In this present life I was born with this knowledge, and through the circumstances of my birth and early life, have been given opportunities not only to develop these powers further, but also to put them to the test —to prove to myself and thousands of other people the truth of the principles given to me in those early days when I was known as 'Minesta.'

Memories of those days were awakened after I had followed the directions of a discarnate American Indian friend who first introduced himself as 'White Eagle.' Some time later White Eagle told me that in an incarnation in South America he had been called 'Hah-Wah-Tah' and had been my father and teacher. Through White Eagle's help and guidance much of my mediumistic work in this incarnation has been accomplished.

An American Indian once told me that according to Indian legend the name White Eagle means 'a spiritual teacher.' 'The white eagle flies straight towards the sun,' he added. A white eagle is also the symbol of the new Age of Aquarius and of St. John, just as the fishes are the symbol of the past Age of Pisces. In the Ancient Mysteries the white eagle was a symbol for the higher psychic and spiritual powers of man, indicating one who had clear sight (clairvoyance) into the inner and secret worlds.

We believe that White Eagle once had an incarnation as an American Indian, a Maya chieftain. Indeed this is the usual personality through which he presents himself to us, but he has become familiar to others of his friends as a Tibetan, an Egyptian priest and Pharaoh, as a humble brother in an obscure order, and an alchemist in the Middle Ages. He also had an important incarnation in France, where the symbol of the six-pointed star was used by the particular brotherhood he served. In Greece, as well as in Egypt, he lived as a teacher and philosopher. As a North American Indian he reached a great age; and according to his own story was a chief among the Six Tribes. His mission then was to lead the Indians into brotherhood and peace among themselves. But whatever bodies and personalities have been his, he always remains to us 'dear old White Eagle.'

White Eagle has never been known to speak harshly or unkindly to anyone; never to judge or condemn; never to speak fearfully or pessimistically, but always hopefully, gently and lovingly. Also he speaks with quiet conviction, with deep understanding of human needs, proving by the quality and depth of his knowledge that it comes from a highly evolved being. He himself makes no such claim, for he reiterates that he is only an instrument, saying 'Only God is good, and He it is that doeth the work.' Although he has been speaking through me now for some forty years, his message has been consistent throughout and a whole way-of-life for mankind has been outlined.

In the closing chapter of *Plumed Serpent* is a description of the last vision I remember during that particular incarnation. I was being admitted into a ceremony in an Indian temple high in the Andes. There I was shown how in years to come people on earth would reach a stage in their evolution when they would not only be ready to welcome but hungering for knowledge about their latent psychic powers. They would reach a point on the journey of life where the mind and intellect would come to cross-roads; when churchianity would be out-worn and a new approach to the mystery of life and of God its Creator would be vitally needed. It was then that I was told by the Master who had taught, tested, and initiated me into these secrets, that I would serve mankind, and with the help of the Great White Brotherhood be permitted to help humanity to save itself from its own dilemma. He said that human salvation lay in the unreleased power within man's own soul, actually the Christ power, which when used correctly could *alone* save him from the ignorance and darkness of a material life.

It is not only *belief* in a higher power that is needed but also *knowledge* of how it works when applied to the way of life. This *is* the salvation of man, by Christ. In mysterious language, still not understood, the whole of the book of the Revelation of John indicates that man himself is the Golden City, the new Jerusalem; and that within him are twelve 'gates' leading into the holy of holies, within the Golden Temple of God. 'Man, know thyself,' were the significant words carved over the archway leading into some of the schools of esoteric learning in ancient days. This knowledge of man's own being is exactly what will be discovered by psychologists and psychiatrists and all students of the mind and soul of man.

But man will need a deeper wisdom than he at present possesses if he is to comprehend the vast implications of his growing knowledge.

The crack in the dark shell of the mortal mind has been made by those who have preceded us into the life to come. While the scientists are pursuing their investigations, a band of people in the spirit world is deeply concerned with the evolution and progress of mankind. This secret body is known as the White Brotherhood, and it has always been the agent of an invisible government and direction working beyond the knowledge and understanding of earthly man. Its work is universal. From these enlightened souls will that deeper wisdom come. To all experimentation on E.S.P. lines there is a limit, but when the 'break through' comes from the *other* side of the dark curtain, the continuation of the life after death in a sunlit world is revealed to earthly man.

II

TOWARDS THE NEW
MEDIUMSHIP

In the early days of communication the adherents of this new belief somewhat rashly asserted that everyone who had become convinced of it should *ipso facto* try at once to develop their own powers of mediumship. Even today we too often hear a clairvoyant giving a message from the Spiritualist platform to the effect that, 'You, sir (or madam), have the gift of mediumship and should be working as a medium,' or 'You have powers of physical mediumship which you should develop,' or 'You have great powers of healing and have guides (naming and describing them) who are waiting to use your powers.' This all sounds promising and to some people flattering, and indeed in some cases it may be quite true; but often such messages lead to disillusionment in practice.

Sometimes people come to consult me who have been reduced to a deplorable state of nervous exhaustion through running to this or that medium's guide, only to get various and sometimes conflicting messages. Messages which seem fulsome or flattering to the recipient, promising great work to come and wonderful gifts to be bestowed, should be regarded with suspicion. Then is the time to 'try the spirits whether they are of God,' otherwise the outcome can be unhappy with a breakdown in health as a possible sequel.

It is not the truths of spirit contact which can prove dangerous, but the many ways these truths can be misused. Discoveries which enhance daily life, such as electricity and (in the future) atomic power, can, like the faculties of mediumship, when used with due care, knowledge and foresight, bring untold blessing into human life; but when misused can result in disaster. Experience has taught me that it can be unwise and even dangerous for the average man or woman to attempt to *force* psychic development without the help of an experienced teacher. But I also know that as part of man's spiritual evolution he should learn to understand and use this most precious gift of God.

We are all born on to this earth with certain natural inclinations which will lead us to follow certain paths. Some of us have been endowed with the gift of music, others find expression through art; others again are born writers, teachers, healers and doctors. The best results will be achieved when children are allowed to work at their own particular vocation. This equally applies to the gift of mediumship. 'Born' mediums are endowed with a special make-up of the etheric* body and a nervous system which will readily enable them to receive impressions from other worlds or, without any particular effort, to see the inhabitants of those worlds, and hear their voices. These people are born 'natural' mediums because at some time during previous incarnations they have undergone special temple-training in the control and use of their faculties. When such a soul returns again to earth seeking incarnation, it will be attracted to parents who can provide the particularly sensitive nervous system and the environment necessary to enable it to unfold its powers. A wise man once said to me, 'Certain people come into this world with the special mission of becoming a medium, a channel between the two worlds. It is important that this should be recognised, for then they will be

* The etheric body is of a finer type of matter and permeates the physical as water does a sponge. It is fully described in Chapter III.

treated with more respect and wisdom by those who can appreciate and understand the sacredness of their calling.' In ancient times the medium (or oracle as he or she was then called) was sent to the temple in childhood for protection, and to provide the best possible conditions for development. This is indicated by the following quotation taken from Manly Hall's *Masonic, Hermetic, Cabalistic and Rosicrucian Philosophy*:

'For many centuries during its early history virgin maidens were consecrated to the service of the oracle. They were called the Phœbades or Pythiœ and constituted that famous order now known as the Pythian Priesthood. It is probable that women were chosen to receive the oracles because their sensitive and emotional nature responded more completely to the "influences." '

In our work at the White Eagle Lodge* we are constantly receiving requests for help from people who have innocently allowed themselves to become obsessed by an entity which has become attached to their aura and from which they cannot get disentangled; it can happen even to well-meaning inquirers who have

* A religious Charitable Trust founded by Grace Cooke in 1936.

ignorantly put themselves under the influence of mischievous entities from the other world. These cases may be slight or extremely severe.

Some have been caused by sitting for too long, and far too often, to obtain automatic writing, or with the planchette or ouija-board,* sitting perhaps every night and in some cases many times during the day as well. They have allowed themselves to become so fascinated by the practice as to become obsessed by it. All these crude methods are dangerous, not only because the operation itself can in time become a compulsion most difficult to control, but also because in the process astral entities are attracted to and obsess the medium: this form of obsession usually develops into a babble of voices which cannot be silenced, continually sounding within the would-be medium's head. For instance, I knew a woman who undoubtedly showed signs of mediumship, but she lacked the mental stability necessary to control the gift. In spite of my frequent warn-

---

* An 'ouija' is a board painted with all the letters of the alphabet. In each of the top corners is painted 'Yes' and 'No.' On the base of the board are numbers up to ten, and in the centre bottom the word 'Goodbye.' A triangular piece of wood (as described for the planchette) is used by means of the sitter's hands resting lightly upon it. Through this contact the spirits guide it to point to any letter or number on the board to make up words and sentences.

ings and attempts at discouragement, she persisted in seeking messages by means of an ouija-board. However often her ouija-board was removed and burned, she obtained another. At a later date she told me that so great was her compulsion that even when riding in a bus she could feel the entity attached to her urging her to spell out messages by mentally picking out letters in the advertisements and forming them into words, while imagining her fingers were moving on the board towards the appropriate letters.

Eventually she was taken to a mental home in a state dangerous both to herself and to others, and not until some months had passed was she allowed to go home, a sadder and a wiser woman, who never touched the ouija-board again.

Another form of obsession I have seen has been brought on by sitting in an unsuitable and inharmonious 'open' or public developing circle, which in the early days of Spiritualism was advocated by some Spiritualist societies as a means of developing one's own mediumship. By trial and error it was discovered that to sit in an open and negative state of mind with the object of inviting all and sundry spirits to take control of a medium was the height of folly.

Most cases of obsession prove to be curable if only the would-be medium will co-operate with the healer; but sad to relate, an innate vanity is often at the root of the trouble, and it is impossible to dislodge the obsessing entity because the victim is subconsciously flattered by the attention he or she is getting and is therefore unwilling to be freed.

Often in such cases the patient, having this streak of vanity in his make-up, has been told that he has been chosen as a special instrument of heaven. This is a great pity, because a day of disillusionment will come, bringing sorrow and regret.

A certain spiritual-healing technique can be employed which will usually dislodge these obsessing entities, by cutting them free from the patient's aura, when they are afterwards taken care of by wiser helpers in the spirit world. If in these cases the healer will analyse the character or nature of the patient, it will usually be found that a weak trait such as resentment, vanity or deep-seated fear is the cause of the trouble, vanity being the most likely.

Those who long to develop their powers of mediumship so that they can comfort the bereaved by giving proof of the after life, should study the subject very carefully before proceeding with their psychic training and development, and feel quite sure that they are meant to do this work. Even then they will be wise to select a reliable group or school of spiritual science and adhere to this one source of training, rather than go from one to another. I cannot too strongly emphasise the risks of unwise practice of communication with disembodied beings who may have no more knowledge of spiritual truth than you yourself have. I want to point to a better way to *real spiritual unfoldment* and contact with the Divine Life. To make the matter quite clear I repeat that apart from the natural or born medium such as I have already described, *every* soul has latent powers which can build an etheric bridge between this life and the next. These powers however should never be forced through psychic development but allowed to develop gradually. A disciplined life of service to others, the practice of meditation, and purity of thought and life—these only are the safe and wise ways.

I fully believe that in time most people will become aware of the close proximity of other spheres of life; and that by striving during this incarnation to unfold their own latent spiritual powers *through meditation and attunement of their soul to the 'Great Light'* they will build into their finer bodies valuable qualities which will be theirs to use in later incarnations.

This does not mean that they will become mediums in the accepted sense. But it does mean that the law of karma* will provide for them exactly those opportunities (physical, mental and spiritual) for which they have worked faithfully during previous incarnations.

How can we tell if we are born a natural medium? I think the answer is that the gifts of a born psychic are apparent in childhood. A natural medium is born with inner vision at one level or another. It is not a power which is sought or developed, but an instinctive awareness of unseen influences outside intellectual cognition. This extra-ordinary power usually displays itself in early childhood and indicates that the soul has come back to earth with its

* The meaning of the Indian word 'karma' is quite simply the continuing action of cause and effect. In other words, with all our actions we put into operation a train of events. St. Paul says, 'Whatsoever a man soweth, that shall he also reap.' We can see this law constantly demonstrated in everyday life. For instance, if we put our hand into a fire it is burnt; if we throw ourselves into water and cannot swim, we may drown; if we break the laws of our country we may go to prison. It is even more certain that if we break any spiritual law we shall suffer. However, if we obey the law of God as stated by Jesus, 'Thou shalt love the Lord thy God with all thy heart . . . and with all thy mind; and thy neighbour as thyself,' we are sowing the seeds of good karma from which we shall reap a good harvest, and incidentally make quicker progress on our path of spiritual evolution.

psychic powers awakened. In such a case, circumstances will invariably guide the medium into the 'planned' channel for his or her life's work. Knowledge and training of these powers will considerably enhance them, and will enable the medium to use these powers in the service of humanity.

A soul comes to physical birth bringing with it a set of lessons to learn (its karma) together with particular attributes acquired in a previous physical existence, which again are to be used to help it to progress. In accepting this truth, we can also recognise the fact that special gifts acquired during a former life and brought back in this, can be enhanced by training. An actor, for instance, may be born with an aptitude for his craft because in his soul lies the memory of what he has learnt of acting in the past; but his technique can be vastly improved by further knowledge and training of his art. The same applies to a musician, an artist, a writer or scientist, and also to the medium, who is born with such aptitudes because the knowledge has been impressed on to the soul during previous experience; but like the artist in whatever branch, the medium must be trained how to control and use this gift.

III

THE ETHERIC BODY AND
THE WINDOWS OF THE SOUL

I recently saw on television a programme of great interest. Four eminent surgeons were interviewed, each being asked if, having seen many people die, and seen death draw close in many other cases, they had formed any views as to whether the soul of man lived on after death. All four expressed belief in an unknown Power which they did not attempt to define, but with regard to human survival, they simply 'did not know.' One surgeon qualified his view, however, by saying that he had on occasion seen patients thought to be 'far gone' with so-called incurable diseases (including cancer) make miraculous last-minute recoveries altogether beyond his power to explain. He had thought at such moments that something within the patients themselves, some 'mental' power, had produced an effect on the *ductless glands*, and through this, a miraculous healing took place.

If an eminent surgeon can testify in this manner regarding the inexplicable healing of some so-called 'fatal' disease, then this opens up a field of research into the possibility that these ductless glands are also sensitive to unseen mental and spiritual influences. There is no doubt that *thought* can have a strong effect on the psychic centres. If the thought of some living person, doctor or healer, can affect the health and chance of recovery of the patient, via the ductless glands, it is logical to believe that communication from another plane or level of life-consciousness can be registered by a medium in the same way. In other words the strong thought-power projected by a communicating spirit can be impressed on the brain of the medium via the etheric body and the nervous system, which forms the medium's 'etheric bridge.'

If true and clear messages are to come from spirit they can only be sent on a perfectly attuned line of communication. Every sensitive or medium through whom transmission is made is highly-strung, with a delicate nervous system. They are sensitive to the thought-waves and impressions of others and very often spontaneously 'pick up' messages from people living in an etheric or soul world just outside the physical. In other words those worlds *insist* on drawing attention to themselves.

To me it seems very important that every inquirer or truth seeker into the life beyond should in the future gain some understanding of his spiritual make-up, and of the fine nervous balance required on the part of the medium before any reliable demonstration of mediumship, public or private, can be achieved.

As I have already said, 'Man, know thyself and thou shalt know God and the Universe,' were the words carved in stone over many of the temples of the Ancient Wisdom; but unfortunately man in this so-called enlightened age still remains extremely ignorant of the mysteries of life and death and of his own being. However, sages and wise men of all ages have learnt about the mysteries through the study of man's own body and soul. In this same study I myself have been greatly helped by the companionship and wisdom of White Eagle.

In the description of the human soul and its potentialities which follows, I am largely quoting from White Eagle's teaching.

'What is the soul? It is the higher self, the invisible temple or clothing of the spirit which has been in construction ever since the spirit was first breathed forth from God. It is as it were the store-house of memories of all the experiences of the past, for as we strive and evolve through each succeeding incarnation, so we are building, by our habitual thoughts and emotions, that beautiful soul, eternal in the heavens.

'The organism through which man contacts his higher self, his soul, is the *etheric body*. This etheric body is not the soul; it is not the astral body, nor is it the mental or the celestial body and it is not the spirit. It is an exact replica of his physical body but composed of finer substance. It interpenetrates the latter and is closely connected with the nervous system.

'At each point in the physical body at which the ductless glands are situated is a corresponding centre or vortex of nervous or psychic force in the etheric body. Through these centres and the etheric body, the physical body gains an inflow of its life force. The etheric body also forms the bridge which enables him to contact after-death states and the higher worlds—a bridge between the physical and the spirit life.

'To the clairvoyant the centres will appear in the aura of an ordinary person like discs of dull light. By the size and appearance of these discs or centres, a clairvoyant may assess the spiritual and psychic state or condition of the individual. Each psychic centre or chakra is also related to its particular plane in spirit life—related either to the lower astral, to the higher astral, the mental, the higher mental or even the spiritual or celestial. So when the soul becomes especially attuned to one or other of these planes, the brightness of the centre or chakra concerned indicates the particular plane in the spirit world to which it is attuned.

'As well as a dense etheric body, man also possesses a finer, which can be seen as a body of light. *This is the soul body* which, as we have said, is a creation not of present physical birth, but of lives in ages past. In other words, into this soul body are woven the experiences and memories of its own past together with those acquired during its sojourn in higher worlds and higher planes of being. It is the permanent part of man, whereas the lower etheric, being closely related to the physical body, as a rule disintegrates shortly after death.* Were it not for the denser or lower etheric however, mortals would get no connection with the soul or with other worlds, for, as we have said, it is the "bridge"

* Sometimes however this does not disintegrate immediately and is known to linger about a home, or buildings, fields, gardens, or churchyards; this is sometimes called a wraith or ghost, but is not the true self. A ghost is therefore an etheric emanation left behind by the physical body and can survive for quite a long time, keeping close to earth. Usually it soon disintegrates.

between the worlds. Following a blow or shock to the brain and nervous system, the soul-consciousness is often driven out, which means the point of contact between the soul and body has been broken for the time being and the latter lies unconscious.

'Communication with all levels of spirit life is made via the nervous system and the etheric body through the main nervous centres or plexuses called *chakras* which we have described. There are three main levels of communication or transmission from the worlds beyond:—

(i) the *astral* from which comes communication from those in the immediate after-life;

(ii) the *higher mental* from which communications often come in the form of symbols and geometric figures;

(iii) the *spiritual* or *celestial* by the method of stimulating the receptive spirit and divine energy of the recipient.

'The *chakras* or etheric centres most used are: for the astral, the solar plexus; for the mental, the throat and brow; while the celestial transmission comes through the heart and crown of the head centres.'

You have no doubt found that from time to time the various messages which you have received from the same person in the spirit world vary in character, and have wondered why this is. It happens because each chakra is related to a particular plane of consciousness, and any one of the chakras of the medium can be used by the communicator to get a message through. Thus the message can vary in character according to which chakra of the medium is being used. For instance, if it is the solar plexus, the message will consist largely of earthly memories. If the throat centre is used, the message will be of a mental nature, and if the brow or head centre, it will be illuminative. If the heart centre, it will be a blending of the nature of all the other chakras. The attitude of both the medium and the sitter will affect the communicator's attempt to get his message across, and if they are harmoniously attuned the better chance there will be of a clear and true communication.

'The seven chakras are situated at the crown of the head, the brow, the throat, the heart, the spleen, the solar plexus, and the genitals or kundalini. These chakras are all animated from the central "power station" in the being of man, which is the heart. When the spiritual forces are flowing into the developed heart centre (developed through love—love of

God and love of man); or when love, or spiritual force, is flowing into the heart centre at
times of prayer or spiritual ecstasy, it flows on
into the other chakras and they in turn light up
—sometimes very dimly, sometimes not all of
them—until they look rather like the little
lights that you put on the Christmas tree. This
is exactly what we ourselves, or a clairvoyant on
your earth, might see; then perhaps the lights
will flicker, fade or go out. Everything is then
shut down. This occurs when there is disturbance by noise, or mental criticism of a destructive nature, and then the term "the conditions
are broken" is used. You see the importance of
worship from the heart, of love for God, for the
beloved soul who is striving to come back?
Such love is an aspect of God, divine when it is
true and selfless. If the feeling is selfish, it is no
longer of God, and then the heart chakra is not
animated; so a different state prevails in the
aura and in the whole being of the sitter hoping
to receive the communication.

'All the power that man needs to foster his
awareness of the spheres from the humblest to
the highest lies within his own being; but we
would emphasise the delicacy of the communication. Earthly people are still ignorant of the
laws which govern communication; they do

not realise how easily the contact can be broken or thrown off balance. For instance, when a medium is in what you call a "state of trance" she is in a most sensitive mental and nervous state, where every sound and movement is greatly amplified. What may appear to be a very slight sound or movement can shock the soul body of the instrument, now outside the body. That soul feels a violent vibration. An instrument for the spirit people has not only to be very delicately poised, but also know how to protect the nervous system from harshness.

'In the olden days such instruments (we prefer that word to "medium") were usually trained as priests or priestesses, and were to a degree removed from the everyday world, living in seclusion, peace and meditation for a period. When this period was over, they would be allowed to go out into the world if desired; but even then the life of everyday was not allowed to interfere with the life of the temple. Those used as instruments today for communication from the higher realms of life will again be secluded and protected in course of time, as man learns to respect the mission of mediumship.'

IV

THE NATURE OF MEDIUMSHIP

I want to make it clear that there are different forms of communication from the spirit world. Some come through on a more violent vibration from a plane near the earth. Often a materialisation seance will be preceded by rather exciting music and a lot of talking, which makes the vibrations coarser, cruder. People say it is a 'happy' atmosphere. This may be good, but it is a happy *earthly* atmosphere, and on that vibration only communications of a very human and earthly nature can come through.

To produce this kind of phenomenon, a physical substance drawn from the life forces of a living body *must* be used. *To make contact with any world or sphere of life, the physical, etheric, mental or celestial substance of that particular plane must be used.* For example, before a disembodied spirit can knock on physical matter, some form of physical substance is needed to make the impact, and spirits themselves discovered this substance to be in the human body. They were taught by superior discarnate intelligences how to use it for this purpose in order to attract the attention of people living on the earth. They made use of a material called ectoplasm, drawn from the lower etheric body but substantial enough to have been measured and weighed by a Dr. Crawford in Ireland, who made many different experiments with a medium named Miss Goligher. He discovered that the material, 'ectoplasm,' was exuded from a medium's mucous membranes. Photographs of it have also been taken by Dr. Glen-Hamilton, of Canada, showing it exuding from the mouth and nostrils of a medium in a stream of white substance not unlike cotton wool. Dr. Crawford also photographed it projecting from the solar plexus like a thick white rod. It was from this material that communicating spirits were able partially to materialise a hand, which enabled them to manipulate physical matter—for example, to move a table, or to rap on it. The earliest intelligent communications from the life beyond came in this way.

So-called 'physical' mediums possess an etheric body which is particularly loosely knit, like coarsely woven material, and because of this the ectoplasm flows from it more freely. On the other hand, some people have a closely woven or tight etheric body, which is not easily used for materialised communications between the two states of life. Nevertheless, another kind of contact can be made with these people by the communicating spirit, at their mental level, through the power of thought.

The psychic power is stronger in people who live close to nature, and are in contact with the nature elementals which live in an etheric world. As we have said, the etheric body of a physical medium is loosely put together and easily drawn upon; but when the intellect becomes very strong, the etheric body seems to shrink, gets tighter, contracts, and when this happens the person becomes averse to all psychic things. The frontal mind dominates, and so such a person appears to be all intellect.

Here again is what White Eagle has to tell about different kinds of mediumship.

'In materialisation (that is when a form resembling someone you know is built up for you to see with your physical eyes) the substance is drawn from the etheric body of the medium, and in degree from the sitters, through the mucous membranes. It is always the etheric body of the medium which is used to produce a materialisation of a spirit, and if any mark is made on the materialised form, such as marking the palms of the hands of the materialising spirit with a colour for instance, with the idea of proving the materialisation to be a fraud, the colour may be found on the physical hands of the medium after the seance. This might suggest to anyone with insufficient knowledge of psychic phenomena that the medium was a fraud, but this is untrue. Any injury or mark inflicted on the etheric body of the medium can mark the physical body also.

'The substance used to manipulate the table, and to make raps or to move objects in physical manifestations, as already explained, is drawn from the etheric body which in turn is closely related to the nervous systems of the sitters and medium. The substance used for this kind of manifestation is identical with the substance from which the little people, the little elementals, are created. So when they see the substance of their own world being used, they "jump to it," for it can provide great fun—for them; they see what is happening and may like to have a game, for they always try to imitate humans.

'We do not for one moment say that you cannot get true messages through physical mediumship; true communications can and *do* come through in this manner, but such methods are not very reliable. It is therefore better for you to know exactly how this sort of communication is operated and the possibility that elementals may intrude. Even entities wandering on the lower astral may see a chance of obtaining a little amusement and take advantage of it—and of you. Can you blame them? So caution is needed, also common sense and discernment.

'In direct voice circles ectoplasm is drawn from the mucous membranes of the medium's throat and nasal organs and used to create an etherealised larynx and apparatus of speech. Although the voice will speak from anywhere in the room or through a trumpet, it *originates* from these partially materialised organs of speech; and as well as having etheric substance from the medium in it, it can be influenced by the medium's mind. This type of phenomenon is always blended and linked with the medium. There can be no such thing as direct (or independent) voice in any exact sense. So-called "direct voice" is always associated with ectoplasm drawn from the mucous membranes of the medium's body, and therefore because the medium's thoughts, feelings and desires are incorporated in the ectoplasm* a certain amount of the medium's make-up will be in that voice.

'You have asked us what happens when someone is doing automatic writing. It just depends what is meant by the term. True automatic writing takes place only when the hand is held and controlled by a partially materialised spirit hand. When the writing is truly automatic, a spirit hand is materialised and placed over the physical hand so that the spirit is actually guiding the writing, but this phenomenon is rare.

'Another type of writing comes largely through the mind and is sometimes called "automatic." We do not say that this type of writing necessarily originates from the subconscious mind of the medium, but there is always the chance that the subconscious of the medium might influence it. It is possible also for a mischievous influence to creep in and cause the message to go wrong. We are sorry to say these things, but we want you to realise

* An investigator once much enlarged a picture of the ectoplasm drawn from a photographic medium who was also a dog fancier and devoted much of her time and interest to this occupation. The ectoplasm was shown to contain forms of countless dogs of all sorts of breeds, indicating the close relationship between the mind and the ectoplasmic substance used from this particular medium's body when obtaining a spirit photograph.

that man's earthly mind can and does unconsciously write down a message sent by a mischievous spirit influence. On the other hand,
pure thoughts may flow from the guide and
teacher of the medium through the medium's
higher self. Messages of this nature through *so
called* "automatic" writing (more correctly it is
inspirational writing) will be true and good,
untainted by the medium's lower self. They will
not mislead, but will inspire with their simplicity, humility and love, and will teach the
operator the truths of life. Always, however,
beware of any message which issues orders,
saying, "Do this! Do that! Go here! Go there!"
The true teacher does not work in this way.
There is so much to learn; so much discernment is necessary. Of course when children
begin to walk they are apt to tumble down.
You do not say because they tumble they must
never walk. It is much the same with psychic
phenomena. There are certainly pitfalls; but
you must learn by experience and by the experience of those who are qualified to teach you.

'You will say that even when this writing
is actually being controlled by a hand materialised from the etheric body of the medium there
is still the possibility of intrusion by the
medium's influence. Yes, this is true; but if the

mind is attuned to the higher self, and the motive is pure, and if what is written is good, true and helpful, does it matter whether it comes from the medium's higher mind or from a spirit guide?

'The solar plexus is the centre used in certain types of clairvoyance and clairaudience. Some people tell you that they can "see" on to the astral plane but only spasmodically. They say, "Often we cannot see when we try, but occasionally we suddenly see a spirit as clearly as we can see you." That is spontaneous vision, which comes like a flash. Such a vision originates from the "eye" of the solar plexus chakra, and is not the same as the trained clairvoyance of someone who by an effort of will has consciously developed and brought into use the higher chakras of heart, throat and head. In other words, this spontaneous clairvoyance is the reflection of an image on the astral plane on to the solar plexus. The fact that a man or woman is able to see either etheric or astral forms does not mean that he or she possesses great knowledge or is highly developed spiritually, but that the solar plexus is particularly open and reflects an image as a mirror does. An open and sensitive solar plexus sometimes results in obsession, for all uncontrolled voices are heard through this centre. So also when people say they are clairaudient they may only be receiving vibrations from the desire world, the plane of the lower and not the higher emotions.

'But there is another type of clairvoyance. Clairvoyance is truly *clear* vision. This does not necessarily mean seeing forms of people on another plane of life. True clairvoyance is vision into the heaven worlds, a revelation and understanding of the mysteries and the laws of spiritual life. Clairaudience also is clear understanding, clear hearing not through the solar plexus but in the heart centre. In the physical forms of manifestation which have been described, the three lower chakras are used; but in the *true* clairvoyance and clairaudience, which develops under direction of the divine will in the person concerned, the three higher are used —the triangle of the heart chakra, the throat and the crown of the head.'

White Eagle says, 'There are various degrees of trance control. We understand from our own use of this human instrument that the trance state is a partnership. Although in some cases it would appear that the spirit or entity controlling a medium is holding the medium's mind in a hypnotic state and taking possession of the whole body, nevertheless it seems to us much more like a partnership, a rising up of the soul of our co-operator in trust, in confidence and in surrender to the communicator. Then, when the medium surrenders to the controlling entity, her personality goes into abeyance, and the discarnate personality takes control. This is done by the powerful projection of our thought through the chakras and therefore through the human nervous system. As we have told you, communication between our world and yours is a very delicate matter, and can easily be thrown off its balance. The nervous system of the medium is easily impaired unless proper care is taken, which means care of the health, care of the living conditions, but it also requires care of the soul and spirit of the instrument.

'Where does the personality of the instrument go when she is in trance? Her personality is not functioning here. Her soul is withdrawn to a higher state. Nevertheless, so close a connection exists between her and the physical condition that if anything were to happen that she did not like, she would at once return to her body. When she is in trance she is raised in consciousness, and what takes place during a trance lecture is recorded by her soul in that higher state of consciousness; but on returning to the body the memory is obliterated. Later perhaps, as the impression gradually filters through to her conscious mind, she may wonder vaguely, "Where have I heard that said before? Was it in a dream?" Some things come as an inner knowing, an inner awareness. But supposing we wish to sponge out completely the memory of something private and intimate, then we can esponge the memory so completely that the medium recalls nothing. It is like pulling down a shutter.

'There is little difference in the mechanism used in deep trance and light trance, but in deep trance there is much more submission to the spirit, a more complete surrender of the medium. During a light control it would seem there is some reluctance on the part of the instrument to surrender completely, so the withdrawal of the medium is incomplete.

'Another point to explain is the difficulty of holding these lines of communication; and here is where conditions sometimes get broken, when there is disturbance or noise or a violent or inharmonious mental intrusion. It requires much practice to hold the line firmly when so little can break the contact.'

White Eagle has explained that there is a

deep attunement between the soul of the spirit guide and that of the medium through whom he is to work. The two are linked by a spiritual law which is universal and governs all life. The spirit guide having been attached and attuned to the medium before in past lives, they are drawn together as steel to magnet.

When White Eagle was once asked *how* he was able to speak with the vocal organs of a human instrument, his answer was this:— 'The human instrument I use was related to me during past incarnations and has been trained through many lives to become my mouthpiece. There is complete harmony and at-one-ment between operator and instrument. When a communication is to be given we draw close to her and speak into a golden disc of light which we see at the back of her head—it might be likened to an etheric microphone built out of substance extracted from the human soul and the physical nervous system. This "etheric microphone" is built of matter of a higher frequency than physical matter and is therefore invisible to the human eye. We draw very close to the human instrument and concentrate our thoughts on this golden ball or disc of light and so our thoughts are transformed into the spoken word.'

Before trance control can be properly established, a degree or *quality of consciousness* must be gained by the medium. This development will be assisted by the spirit control, possibly without the medium's being aware of what is happening. It may take years before the medium learns how to raise the consciousness from the physical to the higher-mental or spiritual level. This degree of trance control is gradually brought about by the infusion of the higher mind of the medium by the personality and spiritual quality of the controlling guide; a very subtle process which gradually evolves and perfects the mediumship.

Occasionally, if the medium's mind is still in a state of activity, it has first to be cleared and subdued by 'their' controlling power; and this is induced by a kind of hypnotism made possible only by the submission and co-operation of the medium.

This form of mediumship will become far more developed in the future, and in due time attunement between spirit guide (or Master) and medium will become so perfect that the medium will be able to hear what is said, and be able to transmit the message almost word for word.

Another aspect of trance mediumship is

used on occasions for transmission of direct messages from friends recently passed into the spirit world. Here I would describe the trance as being more like an 'influence' or remote control. This means that the medium will often unconsciously take on the mannerisms or characteristics of a communicating personality, and is unquestionably strongly influenced by it, although unaware of this. Some very fine and telling evidence has been received through this form of remote control.

Sometimes the miracles and parables of Jesus are cited as instances of the practice of mediumship. I myself believe that Jesus was endowed with extraordinary powers, but would not claim that they come within the scope of what would today be described as mediumhip. He had attained mastership over physical matter. The result was complete control over himself—a state only to be attained through self-discipline and self-mastery over a long period of time. This state cannot be compared with that of an ordinary medium.

It is sometimes suggested that mediumistic controls are not necessarily separate beings, but can be described as secondary personalities or creations of the subconscious mind of the medium. About this White Eagle says:—

'This is a delicate subject and we would not like to be reported inaccurately. But there *are* cases where the medium creates a thought-form and that thought-form becomes animated; or in other words it becomes real enough to be seen and described by a young clairvoyant who has not learnt how to differentiate between a thought-form and a living spirit. Such forms can be very active and the medium's subconsciousness can in all good faith give forth messages purporting to come from a highly evolved spirit entity, when in reality it stems from such a thought-form.

'In the book *The Return of Arthur Conan Doyle*, Sir Arthur spoke of the various personalities which the soul had adopted during its former incarnations. We ourselves have referred to them as being like clothes or dresses left hanging in the wardrobe. These dresses can be taken out and used again. Sometimes you will have a "guide" described and will say, "I am very happy to know my guide." At another time someone else describes yet another guide, so apparently you have two guides. Later on you may have a third guide described. By this time you are a little confused. All these descriptions may refer to the one spirit, who, according to the conditions prevailing at the time, will clothe himself or herself in garments of one or other of his past incarnations. A guide presents himself or herself in clothes or outer bodies of different nationalities according to the particular vibration on which he is working at a given time. So it is with a medium, for the medium also has had past incarnations. This applies to every one. You yourself may feel sometimes that you are being overshadowed, perhaps by an Eastern influence, quiet and contemplative. You may ascribe that to your guide, but it is possibly an extension of your own soul life.

'So, to answer the question we say, Yes, it is *possible* that the influences or entities coming through the medium may be an extension of the medium's own soul, but not in all cases.

'After all, does it matter greatly whether the voice that is speaking is a separate entity? What matters is whether that voice is giving you something which is pure and elevating, if it is helping you to rise above the darkness of earth. Even if it does come from your own higher self does it matter? Here is the real point. We feel there is a little too much docketing, too much putting into separate pigeon-holes, about these things. Whatsoever is good and true and beautiful, accept and ponder in your heart. We hope we have answered the question. Yes, it is possible that so called controls can be either thought-forms created by the medium or an extension of the medium's own soul, but they are more often separate individuals come to earth from the Great White Lodge in order to help mankind out of a state of darkness.'

V

PREPARATION FOR MEDIUMSHIP

Once we feel assured that psychic development is right for us, how should we set about unfolding and developing any soul potentialities we may possess? So many 'rush in where angels fear to tread' and later have cause to repent and lament. However, others born to the mission of mediumship and possessing undoubted psychic power will, if earnest and sincere, be guided to find a wise instructor. In most cases, this is the first essential for the training of mediumship. To take part in an open circle, where all the others are equally ignorant of the subtleties and the mechanics of mediumship, is more than foolish; it is dangerous.

So, if you feel you want to develop psychic and spiritual powers, first of all study every possible angle of the subject, and put yourself on a good foundation. 'Know thyself' and learn the intricacies of human nature. Use common sense and at the same time be wise and humble enough to listen to advice from the more experienced. The young medium must try to discard arrogance and egotism. He must discard messages with any taint of self-importance or flattery of himself or the spirit messenger, and accept only those which to him contain an authentic ring of truth, and are without condemnation of others. No good, true guide will ever prognosticate evil happenings. His vision is always centred upon the good or God, the true and the beautiful. 'By their fruits ye shall know them,' said the Master Jesus and St. Paul added, 'Try the spirits whether they are of God.'

Training of a medium should include preparation on each plane, physical, emotional, mental and spiritual. Development is not just a matter of remaining passive and surrendering the mind and emotions to any extraneous influence. This practice is highly dangerous. Knowledge of the 'mechanics' of mediumship is required, but the preparation for its development should be based on good physical health, mental balance and spiritual aspiration.

In *every* form of mediumship the physical body of the medium is used, for communications from the spirit and soul world must necessarily come via man's etheric or soul body, his nervous system and brain. Therefore good health must be the basis of a medium's training, since the physical organism reflects on to the etheric plane. The word 'automatic' is often used in connection with communication from the spirit life; for example—automatic writing, spontaneous messages and spontaneous clairvoyance. Communications of this kind may come to the natural psychic who by chance 'tunes in' to the right 'wave length;' but this ability to 'tune in' must be under the medium's control and most mediums need to be prepared and trained, the physical organism disciplined. Some people, even in ordinary human ways of expression, are really inhibited because of ill health or some handicap. Much the same applies to the power of expression of a spirit communicator, when trying to use as a channel someone who is clogged and congested through unhealthy ways of life.

The digestive and circulatory systems are very much involved in mediumistic practice; therefore to obtain the best conditions it is advisable for all the organs of the body to be functioning harmoniously. Two hours should elapse after taking a meal before any form of mediumship is attempted. One cannot concentrate harmoniously upon the spirit and a spiritual state of life when one is, say, in discomfort due to indigestion or nervous tension.

Purification, then, of the physical organism by discipline is important. This entails a well balanced diet which means sufficient fresh vegetables, cheese, nuts or other fleshless protein, salads, fruit and milk; it also entails abstinence from smoking and alcohol, for the habit of smoking beclouds the aura, while the unwise taking of alcohol can attract undesirable elements from the denser astral planes.

Every aspiring medium should understand the effect of emotional disturbance on his own nervous system and his etheric body. You can demonstrate this for yourself to prove its truth. For if you become emotionally upset you will suffer from indigestion or headaches, neuralgia or neuritis, rheumatism and many such aches and pains. All these symptoms can have their origin in nervous tension resulting from emotional stress. These conditions also inhibit the harmonious circulation of the psychic forces through the nervous system and the ductless glands and of course through the brain; thereby preventing the clear, pure flow of words or ideas coming through from communicators on a higher level.

If you look at a lake or pool of water when it is disturbed by a breeze, all reflections on the surface will be mis-shapen. The soul or psyche is related to the water element and is as easily affected; therefore control of the emotions is essential in mediumship.

Preparation on the spiritual plane of life is achieved through aspiration, meditation and attunement to the Great Light—to God.

The body must be constantly attuned to purer vibrations, by practice of right thinking, by constant worship of the Creator, and by expressing this worship in service to all life. What is right thinking, it may be asked. Perhaps it could be summed up in that one word SERVICE—a desire to work with God, inspired by a Godlike spirit which is LOVE: love to mankind, towards all living creatures; love towards the infinite goodness which pervades all things. With the expansion of consciousness, which ever increases through the practice of meditation and absorption of heavenly precepts, the perfect etheric bridge is built.

A number of mediums, having been thoroughly trained and after much experience, are doing remarkable work healing the sick and comforting the bereaved; or, in some cases, becoming clear channels through whom philosophy and teaching of a high order can come through from the soul world. No matter, however, what the standard of mediumship may be, the person concerned will certainly need additional qualifications before the case for the soul's survival can be presented in the best possible light to the general public. No speaker or medium should appear on a public platform without undergoing preparation and training in public speaking and voice production and projection so that they can present and demonstrate their case clearly and capably.

I say this because many mediums in the past have suffered criticism, misunderstanding and even insult and persecution made all the more hurtful by the fact that they were really giving beautiful, priceless knowledge to the world. This has sometimes happened because the medium has rushed on to the public platform lacking the poise and capacity which public speaking and demonstration of psychic gifts demands.

Anyone who has the power to contact the next world should always seek to present the message in the best possible manner and form; aware that he will often have to deal with suspicious, unbelieving and even antagonistic people whose attitude might understandably enough upset the equilibrium of one so sensitive as a medium must be. Should this happen, any link between the two worlds is at once broken, and the medium will feel hurt and exhausted, and might even become ill as a result. For instance, the famous medium, Mrs. Meurig Morris, during the proceedings she took against the *Daily Mail* for libel against her and her mediumship, was controlled by her guide Power when in court. Mr. Justice McCarthy ordered her to be removed immediately from the court; and as a result of being seized by the usher while in a state of trance, her etheric body received a violent shock, and she was ill for a long time afterwards.

Again, the late famous materialising medium, Cecil Husk, was permanently blinded because an ignorant and suspicious sitter flashed a light on him while he was in deep trance. A friend of mine also suffered for several days from sickness after too hastily breaking away from a direct voice circle and going out into a crowded thoroughfare. She endured pain and uncontrollable vomiting until a healer was sent for, who healed her sickness, and whose guide explained exactly what had caused it. She was told that because she had hurried away so suddenly from the scene, the ectoplasm which she had been giving out had broken off instead of being slowly and harmoniously absorbed back into the solar plexus. This had shocked the nervous system, and the result was violent pain and sickness.

It must be clearly stated that any use of psychic force is a delicate operation which if mishandled can be dangerous to the nervous system. Therefore all psychic sensitives should safeguard themselves by knowledge and preparation against any shocks such as we describe. In bygone days, the oracle (or medium) was treated with great care, respect and even reverence. Before entering any trance state she had to purify her physical body by fasting, bathing, and being re-clothed in sanctified raiment. Speaking for myself, I have found it necessary in trance work to withdraw completely from outer duties and domestic claims and interests, and to remain in my own room in meditation both before, to give time to attune myself to the inner worlds, and afterwards for a period of re-adjustment to the everyday world. Should this be neglected, I suffer from severe headache through nervous stress.

It is important for the medium to learn self-control, balance and restraint. When anyone has received unshakeable and reiterated proof of the soul's survival, and has likewise given such proof many times over to others, he can afford to remain untouched by praise or blame. To deny the mass of evidence which has poured through from the world beyond for over a century is both vain and ignorant.

*   *   *

Mediums are often entrusted with many confidences either before or after a sitting, and should regard these as sacred, and their calling as one of high honour. No one should ever use information gained in confidence from this or any other source for his own benefit, still less to gain power over another person. Mediumship, when practised either professionally or other-wise, should be regarded as a most honourable and indeed dedicated life-service.

Much has been said about mediums accepting fees for their work, most often by people who have never felt much need of money, and who forget that they have been unusually blessed in this respect. Should they not feel the more kindly and tolerant towards any medium who through necessity has to earn money? To use God-given powers unselfishly in order to comfort and help humanity demands a great expenditure of nerve force and strength; and it is as well to remember that while money itself can be a temptation to some people, pride, self-aggrandisement and love of power can tempt others still more.

Some, of course, feel that if any money is handed over, the medium is most likely only working for gain, and for that reason less likely to be reliable; whereas if nothing is paid, it ensures that the message will be true. But mediumship, regarded as a God-given aptitude, comes into the same category as literary or artistic gifts. All these arts are the result of inspiration, and due in some way to contact with the soul-planes of creation, even as mediumship is. Every such gift has to be developed and its possessor trained to use that gift, often over a long period. None would suggest that the fruits of this inspiration and training in the case of the artist, musician or writer should not be paid for, but for the medium to receive money for work is frowned upon.

The medium is not necessarily endowed by providence with a private income, but must be housed, fed and clothed like anyone else. The demands made by the public on a medium usually leave her neither time nor strength enough to earn a living in the outer world. Necessity forces her to accept money for her services; but this of itself does not belittle their value or the value of the truth she is demonstrating, any more than one would decry an artist because one pays to see his work.

As I have already said, the practice of mediumship should be regarded as an honourable profession. In spite of this there *are* those who have used their mediumistic powers to gain popularity or position. This not infrequently happens when they themselves are in comfortable circumstances, and are thought to be all the better mediums for this reason. This does not follow however; any good and well-trained professional mediums who honour their profession can give fine results both in the quality of evidence for survival and in the wealth of knowledge they can impart concerning the life beyond. The individual sitter must use both judgment and discrimination in the selection of the medium he would consult, and, above all, bring with him a loving heart and sympathetic understanding, well aware that contact between worlds is never slick, never facile, and needs the best we all can give.

VI

DISCRIMINATION

In wireless or television reception, or in photography, we accept the fact that unless we follow certain rules no results will be obtained; but when some bereaved person seeks evidence of an after life (for sometimes the sitter is at fault) if such evidence is not forthcoming on the spot (the exact *type of evidence* previously expected by that sitter) then the communications are said to be unreliable and even false. Sometimes a sudden and apparently spontaneous contact can be made when least expected, depending on prevailing conditions, but generally speaking whenever a special appointment is made for a sitting, the best possible conditions should be provided for the communication.

I write from long and sometimes sad experience when I say how little real understanding exists on the part of most inquirers regarding the delicacy of the conditions which should be provided by both medium and inquirer before messages from the 'Other Side' can come through clearly and correctly; and how few of such inquirers ever come to realise that communication is not nearly so simple as many seem to think. Although sometimes it may *look* easy and proves overwhelmingly evidential, at other times it is laborious, the message gets confused and what comes through may be muddled or even misleading, calling for time and patience and earnest study to sort out its meaning; and all this perhaps was due to noise or the jangled mind of the inquirer, or the battery of harsh, materialistic, thought-forces in the surroundings.

For instance, a communicator when coming into contact with an earthly condition is at times unable to remember what he has said when speaking on another occasion through a different medium, and this inaccuracy can cause confusion and doubt. Sometimes, indeed very often, messages come through which are extremely clear, exact and perfectly evidential from an earthly standard, and then the same spirit will show, when speaking through another medium, complete ignorance of what he has said. I think this occurs because of the varying states and conditions prevailing at the time of reception.

The sitter should use his intelligence to

analyse any messages received which give advice that goes against common sense—such as telling the recipient to go (perhaps at great inconvenience) to visit a friend (or even an unknown person) at a distance, or to make some drastic change in his home or employment. Such messages can be misleading and mischievous, and even wreak havoc. By and large, no evolved spirit would ever interfere with a person's freewill choice or force him to make drastic changes in his material life. Any wise spirit knows that people are put here in the physical life to learn lessons which are necessary and good for them to learn; therefore any decisions of vital importance affecting their material affairs must be left for them to decide. This develops character. Only too often people want and expect those on the other side to cross all their 't's' and dot all their 'i's' for them, and to tell them an easy way out of all their troubles. They can indeed give us guidance concerning recognition of and obedience to spiritual law and also what can prove to be astounding evidence, if trouble is taken to study and analyse *exactly* what comes through, and if we can, when necessary, wait patiently for the fulfilment of their message; but they cannot do the work for us.

A guide comes back with but one object: to strengthen the spiritual nature of the person in his charge, and to help by wisdom and love to further that person's own evolution. Constant and pure contact of this nature is assuredly the greatest gift ever offered to mankind; it is for men to learn to accept and use this gift as it was intended, when it can bring nothing but blessing and joy into their lives.

On this subject of discrimination White Eagle says, 'So much filters through from the spirit world which is confused and is not the pure truth, and this can cause a great deal of trouble. Sometimes messages come—even through your own instrumentality—which confuse you and you do not understand, so you ask us to help to unravel these messages.

'Let us make it quite clear that a message from a spirit can descend through the higher and lower astral planes and then through a physical brain to the physical life; but then there is the self-will of the one who is receiving or seeking the message to take into account, and he or she may unconsciously change the message to suit his or her own ideas. All such messages come through on a very fine and subtle wave-length and their meaning can easily become distorted.

'At this you will naturally ask how are you to distinguish between the true and the confused message? Well, you are here in this world to be trained not only by the invisible company, but by the promptings of your own spirit. God has planted within you all a centre of divine truth—literally "the dot within the circle"—and it is from this centre of your being that truth will come. Around that centre, however, a stratum of confusion or illusion has collected, and it is so sad when someone striving to develop his own spiritual powers and knowledge does not understand how easily the messages which come to him can be distorted as they pass through this stratum of confusion.

'You who are aspiring to become instruments have to be trained to make your contact; and you have also to train yourselves, first of all through meditation. We put meditation first for the reason that as you learn to meditate you are learning to raise your consciousness above the astral plane to the higher mental. True meditation takes place on the higher mental plane, and as you practise meditation you become more and more able to fix your consciousness upon this plane and to distinguish it from the confusion of the astral. Even so, how can you be sure that you are reaching that higher mental plane and that you are receiving teaching through one of the higher guides? Well, Jesus gave you the key when he said, "By their fruits ye shall know them." One striking quality of the message coming from a high source is that of humility. You will never find a true teacher making big claims. He will under-state rather than over-state. He is very careful about what he says, and you will always notice a quality of love, humility, gentleness in his conversation.

'Some of the communicators from our world come from the lower astral plane and have little authority for what they say; others are truly the instruments of the Adepts or the Masters. We say again, by their fruits ye shall know the great ones; their keynote is humility and simplicity; they make no great claims of any kind. And when you make contact with them on the higher mental plane, you will do so *by virtue of the spirit of the Christ within your own heart*, which is pure and holy, and wholly true. This is the centre from which all aspirants must work.'

The goal to be reached in mediumship is the conscious development of the God within (man's spirit) which alone can reach out and touch truth on higher levels of life. If a medium, or would-be medium, concentrates on this factor before anything else, and subdues all egotism, it raises him or her above the plane of confusion and self-deception into the pure atmosphere of the spiritual life, to which state the divine spark in man is leading him.

VII

THE WAY OF MEDITATION

The one essential quality in all mediumistic training is love—love of God and His creation. This quality embraces others such as humility, tolerance, sincerity and truth. Yet love without knowledge is not enough; for if you are only sending out love you can fall into a complacent, dreamy state; but with the opening of the higher or head centres you can work with knowledge. Therefore knowledge should be coupled with love. Strive for deeper knowledge; strive ever for a fuller consciousness of all life and also for understanding of what you are doing on these higher planes. Truth within the soul, together with wisdom and common sense, is essential. Once these qualities are developed, there is little likelihood of error. Above all look to purity of motive, a ready desire to accept and obey the divine will or divine law.

A medium must remain untouched by the opinions of other men and must not seek to satisfy and win the approbation of worldly minds. Much harm results from this. Conviction of the truth of another world and of communication with those who inhabit it does not come from the intellect alone. Its motive force is pure spirit, and depends on a simple, pure heart, which desires nothing for itself and offers itself as a human bridge between the living and the so-called dead.

Self-discipline and self-control are therefore of the utmost importance. An early instruction given to me by my teacher was this: 'Before you allow yourself to be controlled or entranced by another entity, you must first learn to control *yourself*. Never allow yourself to be influenced or controlled by any spirit against your will, and always pray that you remain master of your own being.'

Certain agents can stimulate the solar plexus centre, alcohol being one. Astonishing communications can take place when drugs or alcohol are used. Any would-be medium under the influence of drugs or alcohol is in the position of a child set down in a power-house, who turns on a switch, but cannot turn it off. People sometimes so long to get into touch with the other side that they will do anything to achieve their object; and being aware that their natural psychic gifts seem to be stimulated by alcohol, they open themselves to various astral broadcasting stations and through ignorance of the laws of mediumship become obsessed by a conglomeration of simultaneous voices and sounds from the astral plane. It is distractingly noisy on some levels of the astral plane when the instrument or receiver is incorrectly tuned in.

The key to control lies within; it is the Christ power, the word of command, the divine will which is in everyone. If ever you are troubled by obsession in this way, remember that you can help the confused and troubled communicators by mentally talking to them firmly, wisely and kindly; telling them that they must seek their teacher and guide in spirit, and go about their business, which is in higher spheres and not close to the earth.

Let the 'I AM' take control. Many mistake their own desires, their vain wishes, for the 'I AM.' The 'I AM' of course is the God, the Master Christ within, who can arise and take possession of the temple and drive out the money changers and intruders.

I have found that when the student has been well instructed in the ways of discrimination and discernment, the safe way for him to proceed is to enter a class for meditation. This is one of the first steps in the development of mental mediumship and also involves elementary training in control over the mind and the body. Silence and stillness are necessary. Even if no particular or exciting psychic power is demonstrated, the student will develop his soul and higher mind on sound lines, making him less liable to self-deception.

I would recommend three, six or nine as being a suitable number of sitters for a group of this kind. The class should always commence in an atmosphere of harmony, relaxation and peace of mind and soul, and be opened by a prayer. Suitable prayers and themes for meditation will be found in my book *Meditation* which can be recommended as a guide to this simple and safe method for the early development of mediumship. When sitting for meditation, try to use the power of imagery to see through the dark veil of materiality into a spirit-world of perfect life, which will present the most perfect replica of earthly scenes; in other words, etherealise in perfect form your ideal of life.

It may be thought and said that man's imagination can delude and mislead, but properly understood, imagination is a soul quality which is essential to the life and progress of man. Indeed, all creative ability lies in the quality of man's Godlike imagination and without imagination life becomes a dull state. It is, moreover, through imagination that we are able to 'feel' or 'sense' how other people 'feel' in times of grief or acute suffering. Imagination is an important God-given gift to enable man to realise the needs of his fellow creatures. Nothing can be designed or made without imagination, which is actually a creative power. Soul substance in the unseen is moulded into form by the mental power of man, whether incarnate or discarnate. A materialised spirit form is built up by the powerful thought of the spirit and his helpers who wish to create a physical image.

Thought-forms are very active on the astral and mental planes of life, but they can always be distinguished from living people, the latter being lighted from within the heart centre, the seat of the divine spirit or life force.

Meditation is a steady going inwards to discover pure spirit, the centre of all creation. The power of pure spirit—which can only be reached in the innermost sanctuary, the temple of silent worship—can overcome all confusion, all barriers of materiality and negative suggestion of the lower mind or earthly thoughts.

During meditation on pure spiritual life, one faces truth and thereafter can really say, 'I know.'

At this level of consciousness, one is actually living in the spirit life and the spirit world. It is here that loved ones meet again in familiar gardens, lands of happy memories, or perhaps in the ideal of a beautiful music room or quiet sitting room.

In time the student will learn to make contact in his meditation with illumined souls from the Halls of Wisdom in the spirit world, will be guided and taught by them not only regarding spiritual law but also regarding the construction and workings of the etheric and soul body in relation to the physical. More than this, he will slowly develop qualities and attributes which will be an infallible guide in his future work as a healer, wise counsellor and servant of the spirit.

The purpose that should be before you is the gentle and natural development of the three higher chakras, the crown, the brow, and the heart, under direction and impulse of the divine will. This development is helped by the practice of meditation, which if you are faithful will teach you how to bring to life these higher chakras, through which contact with and inspiration from the higher worlds will come.

God is spirit and those who love and worship Him must do so in spirit. Man also is spirit, and those who would commune with the next world must do so in spirit apart from the entanglements of earth and the body of earth. This is the golden chord sounding through all life; and to strike the true note of reunion with loved ones in spirit across the etheric bridge, it is necessary to develop through meditation a consciousness of life in God—and God in life.

I feel I cannot do better than conclude this book with White Eagle's words, which seem to sum up what we have been saying:—

'The higher self is composed of very fine ether and is pulsating with light, which as you develop will begin to shine through the chakras of your being or the "windows of your soul."

'When this divine fire, which is the divine magic, is brought into full operation so that all the chakras are working as God intended, then the whole physical body will be in a state of ascension. We mean by this that the whole physical body, although still of a physical nature, will be functioning on a much higher plane of consciousness than it is at present. At the present time it is in a dark state, but when the divine fire is alive and active, then the body will be raised in vibration and will be light and beautiful, and approaching the standard of the God men, the sun men, who walked this earth in the beginning of its creation.

'Wise and great teachers are drawing closer to the earth to bring their wisdom to mankind. Souls who have passed through the fires of suffering and who have attained to a degree of self-discipline will be taught how *safely* to develop the divine fire within themselves, for this divine fire is both creative and destructive; and the ignorant and the self-willed who think to rush the door of the temple and use the mysteries of creation in a self-willed and selfish way can bring destruction upon themselves. Thus you will see the necessity for self-discipline and careful preparation of the finer vehicles. Those in the spheres of light who watch over mankind, strive to preserve the secrets so that man himself may be prepared and preserved to enter into the full joy of the God life which is the will and the purpose of the Creator.

'Man in his ignorance is all the time dissipating this divine fire, through animalism and passion, through uncontrolled emotion. Every time you give way to passion and temper, you are dissipating this holy and divine fire; and every time these emotions are controlled and transmuted into love, you are building the light into your vehicles. You are using this divine fire to beautify yourself and the world and to glorify God.'

*   *   *

'Meditation is the true way to unfold the spiritual awareness which is deep in the innermost being of man. We do not refer to a mental practice but to an awareness of truth which arises from the heart. It is really the awakening and unfolding of the heart centre, by love. Just as a flower unfolds in the rays of the sun, so the heart centre stirs through daily meditation and practice of divine love. Then a little light begins to shine upon the path of the seeker for God. God does not force you to use this power, but places it within your reach. A price, however, has to be paid by every soul who enters upon the path. That price is the rejection and subjection of all that is coarse, cruel and unlovely in himself. The joy in your life then will be the joy of your spirit, the joy of God's love, God's harmony and beauty. To those who do not understand, this crucifixion of the lower self appears to be a terrible experience; the wise man sees in crucifixion an arising and going forth to meet God, the Infinite and Eternal Spirit, and becoming attuned or at-one with God's universal life stream.

'Develop from the heart, meditate on love, live love, absorb love, give love, and you will become alight with the divine fire. You will have within your hands the divine magic, to heal the sick, to comfort the bereaved, to bless the sorrowful, to beautify everything you touch, and to bring peace and happiness to the life of man.'

THE WHITE EAGLE PUBLISHING TRUST is part of the wider work of the White Eagle Lodge, a meeting place or fraternity in which people may find a place for growth and understanding, and a place in which the teachings of White Eagle find practical expression. Here men and women may come to learn the reason for their life on earth and how to serve and live in harmony with the whole brotherhood of life, visible and invisible, in health and happiness.

Readers wishing to know more of the work of the White Eagle Lodge may write to the General Secretary, The White Eagle Lodge, New Lands, Brewells Lane, Liss, Hampshire, England GU33 7HY (tel. 0730 893300; from April 1995, 01730 893300) or can call at The White Eagle Lodge, 9 St Mary Abbots Place, Kensington, London W8 6LS (tel. 071-603 7914; from April 1995, 0171-603 7914). In the Americas please write to Church of the White Eagle Lodge, P. O. Box 930, Montgomery, Texas 77 and in Australasia to The White Eagle Lodge (Australasia), Willomee, P. O. Box 225, Maleny, Queensland 4552.